Original title:
The Roof of My Memories

Copyright © 2025 Creative Arts Management OÜ
All rights reserved.

Author: Rafael Sterling
ISBN HARDBACK: 978-1-80587-086-9
ISBN PAPERBACK: 978-1-80587-556-7

Beyond the Thatch of Yesterday

In the attic of my mind, things are piled high,
Old shoes and hats, a random pie.
Luggage from a trip that never took flight,
A rubber chicken? Oh, what a sight!

Dust bunnies dance like they're in a race,
Chasing a sock that's lost its place.
An old radio plays a tune out of key,
While I wonder who taught my cat to be free.

The calendar laughs, it's out of date,
It's still stuck in 2008, what a fate!
Birthday wishes scribbled on napkins galore,
Who knew the past could be such a chore?

Yet in this chaos, there's joy that I find,
Memories tickle like a soft friend's grind.
With a grin, I recall the nights spent in mirth,
Beyond the thatch lies a treasure of worth.

Beneath the Gabled Past

In the attic where old dust bunnies roam,
Found a hat I borrowed, but forgot to take home.
A rubber chicken, a joke from my youth,
Tickles my brain, oh, the funny truths.

Old albums filled with hair that was wild,
Mom's crazy perm, how she once looked styled.
Dad's mustache, a furry caterpillar grand,
Now history's laughter, all close at hand.

Shingles of Nostalgia

A squeaky floorboard sings a silly tune,
As I waltz through memories beneath the moon.
Marbles and jacks scattered wide on the floor,
Each little treasure, a tale to explore.

The games we played with laughter so loud,
Imitating astronauts, we felt so proud.
Now grown with jobs, still clutching that prize,
Life's a bit silly, oh what a surprise!

Reflections on a Weathered Surface

The old mirror holds more than a few lines,
Showing my youth with its goofy designs.
A face full of pie from a birthday gone bad,
Laughter erupts, oh, the joyful we had.

Yet here I stand, still trying to grin,
With toothpaste on chin, where do I begin?
Those youthful shenanigans, a comedic grace,
Tickling my heart, oh, time's funny chase.

Attic of Forgotten Dreams

In the attic of dreams, where old toys play shy,
A yo-yo that spun with a determined sigh.
A teddy bear dressed like a pirate so bold,
Guarding the treasure of stories untold.

The capes we wore during superhero quests,
Worn like a badge from our childhood tests.
Yet here we are, still seeking that thrill,
Trading our capes for a four-dollar bill!

The Gables of Yesterday

Up on a peak where laughs reside,
Old socks and snacks, we used to bide.
Every tumble, roll, and silly spat,
Leaves me chuckling, imagine that!

The cat in a hat gave lessons in grace,
Fell off the shelf, oh what a face!
Memories hang like a picture upside down,
In the attic of time, where we dance around.

A Canopy of Pale Reminders

Under a shade made of playful dreams,
Where lemonade spills and laughter streams.
Socks on the line, doing a jig,
Was it a bird or a dancing pig?

Old toys forgotten, yet still they sing,
Stories of mischief, oh what a fling!
The garden's a circus of whimsical sights,
With cucumbers dressed for the fanciest nights.

Skimming Through Fleeting Moments

Pages torn from the book of my youth,
Each scribble a joke, no time for the truth.
Butterflies chased, and ice cream spills,
A slip on the grass gave me permanent thrills.

I wore my dad's shoes, two sizes too big,
Strutted like a star, did a silly jig.
The bubbles I blew floated high in the sky,
Each pop was a giggle, oh my oh my!

The Overhang of Emotion

Beneath a roof that flaps with cheer,
Where every shadow shows us near.
A slip of the tongue, I told my goldfish,
It laughed so hard, it granted my wish!

In pockets of laughter, memories hide,
Like lost marbles, they scatter and glide.
The ceiling sounds giggles from way up high,
A dance of delight that never says goodbye.

Shadows Dancing in Sunlight

In the garden where daisies sway,
My thoughts do cartwheels, come what may.
Lemonade spills, a sight so bright,
Rabbits hop by, giving quite a fright.

Sunbeams tickle my nose with glee,
I chase my past like a lost bumblebee.
With giggles and snorts, memories flow,
The dance of shadows puts up a show.

Timeless Whispers from Above

Socks in the dryer spin tales so grand,
Of days when I roamed with an ice cream stand.
Whispers cascade like leaves in the breeze,
Each laugh a treasure, each moment, a tease.

Look up, my friend, at the clouds overhead,
They carry the secrets that dreams never said.
With smiles as wide as a pizza's round crust,
I gather the giggles; it's all a must.

A Tapestry of Forgotten Tales

In a napping cat's shadow, I find my youth,
A treasure chest filled with nonsensical truth.
Worms in the dirt tell stories they knew,
Of mud pies and laughter and silly shoe stew.

Kites fly above with colors so bold,
They whisper of mischief from days of old.
Each tug at the string, a laugh from the past,
In this thread of tales, my joy holds fast.

When the Moonlight Finds Its Way

Bouncing off walls, light tiptoes at night,
It's a waltz of jokers, oh what a sight!
With jellybeans jiggling, the laughter explodes,
As I spot the raccoon on its sugar-stuffed roads.

Beneath the stars, my childhood leaps,
A parade of giggles that never sleeps.
As moonlight beams down on the antics we shared,
I trip on the sky, but I don't feel impaired.

The Shade of Unspoken Stories

In the attic, dust collects,
Where old hats dance and laugh,
A shoe with a funny complex,
Wonders what it lost in half.

A chair that tells of naps taken,
While a cat spins tales so tall,
Its yarn all tangled, shaken,
In the corner, it's left to sprawl.

Forgotten games in boxy frames,
Carried echoes of our fun,
We played without scoring names,
Guess who hides from everyone?

The shadowy giggles flicker fast,
Against the walls, they tell their tale,
Memories bend and twist, uncast,
In this attic, we shall regale.

Cracks in the Plot of Time

In my mind's eye, I see a dance,
Of memories with missing shoes,
A plot that twists, a funny chance,
As laughter's what it freely woos.

The clock ticks backward now and then,
Grandpa's tales of when he swore,
A goat once drank his inked-up pen,
Which made the stories even more.

A squirrel hoards my favorite snack,
It knows the secrets, oh, so sly,
While I just giggle at the crack,
In time's own plot, I'll never die.

Each moment's like a jester's game,
Where parts of me just float away,
Yet still, they whisper, shout my name,
In silly dreams, we laugh and play.

Soaring Through Tinted Glass

Through windows framed with silly hues,
I spy past giggles, grand, and free,
Old flames of childhood, bright like news,
In gardens where the wild things be.

A kite once tangled in a tree,
That called itself a flying whale,
I watched it dance and laugh with glee,
With stories only winds could hail.

The sun spills colors on my page,
Where sketches of lost friends reside,
In scribbles that defy an age,
With laughter echoing inside.

A rainbow slips, and with a grin,
I know each tint has tales to share,
In every hue where light knocks in,
I find the joy that lingers there.

Forgotten Tracks Beneath the Beams

In dusty corners, whispers roam,
Where my childhood tracks were laid,
A treasure map that leads back home,
To Lego castles, proudly made.

Beneath the beams all creaky, wild,
Old socks with laughter's scent remain,
While crayons bore the dreams of a child,
Now I find them quite insane.

Forgotten toys in battle lines,
Charge at shadows, brave and bold,
While I laugh at their silly designs,
Pretend adventures never grow old.

Each creak of wood has stories here,
Of hide-and-seek in playful jest,
Within these walls, there's little fear,
For now, I wear nostalgia's vest.

Sunlight on a Dusty Path

Sunlight spills on the ground,
Dust dances all around.
Old shoes take a silent walk,
Whispering secrets like a talk.

Cats in shadows seem to play,
Chasing dust motes on their way.
Silly squirrels in a nut chase,
Life's a comedy, full of grace.

Bicycles rust and tires squeak,
A symphony of the antique.
Laughter echoes off the walls,
Worn-out stories, muffled calls.

Sun shines bright, a cheeky grin,
Every puddle's a kookie spin.
Memories twirl, a dandy dance,
Finding joy in every chance.

Chambers of Untold Tales

In the attic, a box sits tight,
Full of treasures, out of sight.
Faded photos, silly hats,
Ghosts of laughter, clever chats.

Socks that vanished, what a shame,
Dusty socks, I miss their game.
They wiggle when I look away,
Play hide and seek, 'til today.

Old typewriters clack with glee,
Typing stories only I see.
Chamber echoes of the past,
Whispers fluttering, oh so fast.

Cobwebs hold their ancient truth,
Hiding echoes of my youth.
Funny moments plastered there,
Caught in time, a jumbled air.

The Breath of Longing Above

Kites fly high in azure skies,
Catching dreams with tiny lies.
They wave like hands that used to cheer,
Innocent hopes that linger near.

Clouds rumble with laughter swift,
Recalling each forgotten gift.
Birds play tag with flapping wings,
Singing tunes of simple things.

The sun peeks through, a playful wink,
Telling tales most dare not think.
Every beam a jolly jest,
Reminders of life's hearty zest.

While stars at night might hide away,
They chuckle softly, come what may.
Chasing dreams, up high we go,
On a journey, just for show.

Hints of History in Each Corner

In the nook, an old chair creaks,
Whispering secrets, laughter peaks.
It rocks with tales of days gone by,
With each sway, a joyful sigh.

Walls adorned with frames askew,
Marvelous mischief in plain view.
Pictures giggle, they once were bright,
Now they murmur in the night.

Books stacked high, a leaning tower,
Each spine boasting of some power.
Pages curl with tales of yore,
Each one opening a door.

Ticking clocks lend time a tease,
Marking moments as they please.
In every shadow, a giggle glows,
Life is a jest that simply grows.

Echoes Beneath the Canopy

Underneath the branches, squirrels hide,
Sharing gossip of the other side.
A pigeon's coo, a butterfly's dance,
Nature's circus, a whimsical chance.

Raindrops tap like a woodpecker's spree,
Soaked socks in puddles, oh woe is me.
Laughter bursts with every splash made,
In this chaos, we've joyfully played.

Memories cling like leaves on a vine,
Every childhood prank, a punchline divine.
Sunbeams flicker like mischievous eyes,
Chasing shadows that dart and surprise.

Caught in the net of a sticky dream,
Where ice cream drips became a big theme.
Laughter echoes in the rustling boughs,
Where time stands still, and joy always bows.

Shadows on the Attic Walls

In the attic room where dust bunnies roam,
Old boxes gather tales of a playful home.
Ghosts of the past whisper through the eaves,
A treasure map made of old jeans and leaves.

Light bulbs flicker, like ideas that pop,
What's in this box? A long-lost mop?
My childhood giggles echo up high,
In the land of forgotten, where old toys lie.

A cardboard castle with a flag made of tape,
King of the mountain, I take my escape.
Fortress of dreams, where dragons still fly,
Beneath the soft glow of the attic sky.

The shadows dance to a rhythm unknown,
Each crack in the wall a side-splitting groan.
Memories line up in a comical row,
In this attic of wonders, laughter will flow.

Whispering Rains of Yesteryear

Pitter-patter on the roof, what a sound,
Each drop like gossip that spins all around.
A bucket below catches tales from above,
Sticky wild stories that we all love.

Rubber boots squish in the puddly spree,
Who knew a storm could bring so much glee?
Paper boats sail on a river of dreams,
Reminding us life is not as it seems.

Dancing in raincoats, we twirl and we dash,
Our laughter erupts with each big splash.
Clouds become pillows, and thunderstorms roar,
In the wild weather, there's always much more.

Leaves slip and slide as we spin to the beat,
Finding joy in a storm, oh what a treat!
Whispering memories weave through the night,
Turning gray skies into pure delight.

Phantoms of Past Skylights

Up in the attic where skylights beam,
Dust motes are dancing, caught in a dream.
Ghosts of old toys twirl in delight,
Whispering secrets from each starry night.

Marbles and trinkets all gather around,
Each one a story, each one a sound.
Jump ropes awaken, swing high in the air,
While shadows of laughter play tag without care.

Painted murals of laughter and cheer,
Sketching their tales, summer's found here.
Time rolls like marbles, through years all aglow,
Painting the past with a comical flow.

Phantoms of giggles, peek from the seams,
We chase them together, in wide-open dreams.
In every moment, we create and explore,
While skylights above keep inviting us more.

Dusty Dreams Above the Ceilings

In a corner, a shoe, makes me laugh,
Was it my style, or just a gaffe?
Lost socks dance with old birthday hats,
Wonders await in the attic flats.

Grandpa's stories, with twists and turns,
A cat on a broom? Oh, how it churns!
A clock that ticks in an entirely new way,
Says it's midnight, but it's bright as day.

I swing from the rafters, a jester's spree,
While dust bunnies grin, just laughing at me.
Each box a treasure, each spiders' web gleams,
Tickling my funny bone, oh the dreams!

With knick-knacks smiling from their own perch,
They whisper secrets from their own church.
Laughter echoes in a whimsical tone,
In the attic of laughter, I find my home.

Skylights to My Yesterdays

Through glass panes, I spy on the past,
Juggling memories like squirrels, so fast.
Trampoline tales bounce in my head,
Where mischief and giggles gloriously wed.

Sunbeams reveal dances once bright,
Where shadows of penguins led me to flight.
A bicycle built for a spirited crew,
Rides through my thoughts, oh, how it flew!

Bedtime stories, all tangled and fun,
Mom's funny faces when day was done.
My childhood's a circus with clowns on parade,
Under skylights where dreams were laid.

Each reflection a slide of a joyful race,
And memories swirl in a whimsical space.
Through dimming light, hilarity beams,
Peeking through skylights, reliving my dreams.

Celestial Thoughts in the Aether

Up high, the stars share a laugh or two,
They wink at each other, like old friends do.
Comets throw parties, glitter in loops,
Jupiter's giggles burst out with whoops!

Galaxies spin with a ludicrous cheer,
While asteroids bounce with a chuckle and sneer.
Nebulas twist in a colorful dance,
Reminding the cosmos life is a chance.

I float on a cloud, sipping on light,
With Martians who boast of their puns so bright.
Between twinkling realms, my heart takes flight,
Drifting through laughter in the starry night.

Cosmic balloons tied to the dream's parade,
Where whimsical wonders are never delayed.
Aether is filled with giggles so grand,
I catch the joy with a starry hand.

The Space Between the Beams

In the beams, a mouse throws a party so quaint,
With cheese confetti that's surely a saint.
Space vacated by dust and playful glee,
Laughing at echoes of joyful decree.

Between rafter shadows, mischief does bloom,
High-fiving the ghosts that haunt every room.
Old hats jump in, to waltz and to spin,
While shadows partake in a whimsical grin.

A dragonfly's whisper is caught in a breeze,
Telling tales of friendship with bees in the trees.
Songs of the past hover soft in the air,
Where laughter and memories dance without care.

In every crevice, a giggle finds room,
With echoes of laughter driving out gloom.
The space is alive, where old tales have swung,
Between the beams, joy continues to spring.

Between the Beams of Yesteryears

Under beams where laughter grew,
A squirrel once wore my old shoe.
Tripped on shadows, fell with grace,
Chased a cat—it ran, I'd chase!

Jars of marbles filled with dreams,
Sock puppets hatching crafty schemes.
Kites tangled high in summer air,
Whispers lost in the neighbor's hair.

Old bicycles with rusty chains,
Each ride a symphony of pains.
Faded comics, pages torn,
Make believe we're never worn.

Underneath that dusty quilt,
Learning rules we never built.
Every laugh a treasured jest,
In the beams, we found our best.

Skylights to What Was

In the light that danced and sparked,
I found a note that said, 'Let's be starred!'
Cookies burnt up in the oven's heat,
A bakery of failure, oh what a treat!

Through skylights peeped a world so wild,
Where every day, I was that child.
Puddles splashed with half-dry schemes,
Turning chores into wild dreams.

Lost a sandwich in a tree,
Came back home as a crumb decree.
Where did the gummy bears all go?
I think they joined the circus show!

Chasing shadows, giggling loud,
Painting rainbows on a cloud.
Those skylights whisper secrets sweet,
Of a time when noses met sticky feet.

Hushed Secrets Amongst the Tiles

Amongst the tiles, whispers roam,
A dance of mice who call it home.
Every crack a tale once spun,
Of washing dishes—who has won?

Hushed secrets in the morning sun,
Granny's cookies, oh such fun!
Flour fights made our mornings bright,
Sticky fingers in the twilight.

Puddles formed from rain above,
Where umbrellas lost their love.
A jellybean launched at the cat,
Now that's a clever diplomat!

Tiles confide in silly sings,
Of little joys and broken things.
Hushed as they keep our secrets tight,
In echoes of our youthful flight.

The Vault of Faded Echoes

In a vault where echoes linger,
I lost a thumb in a sweet finger.
Balloons that hid from the sharp of day,
Then popped—oh, what a silly play!

Faded colors in the night,
Socks that vanished without plight.
A treasure map drawn with crayon bright,
Leads to cookies out of sight!

In the vault of giddy gales,
Pretend ships set off with sails.
A captain with a vegetable hat,
Held court to a nimble cat.

Faded laughter bounces high,
Frogs in bow ties do not comply.
Amongst the echoes, joy remains,
In silly tones and silly pains.

Nostalgia's Attic Archive

In the attic, dust bunnies play,
They dance with old shoes from yesterday.
A bike with flat tires, a bike that won,
Still waiting for rides in the summer sun.

Old photos with hair like a crazy tree,
Grandpa's mustache, quite possibly a bee.
A clock that ticks, but never chimes,
Must've been made in some ancient times.

The board games stacked, with missing parts,
Their rules faded, yet still warm our hearts.
A whoopee cushion with a half-hearted sound,
Lies waiting to prank (if it's ever found).

Glasses from parties where no one could see,
The cake on the table, now sad as can be.
Yet laughter echoes through the dusty pane,
In this archive, joy's never in vain.

Tiles of Reminiscence

On the roof, memories scatter and slip,
Like marbles lost on a starry trip.
A frisbee that flew, then landed so wide,
Next to a cactus that cried and died.

Tiles sing stories of picnics and pies,
Where ants wore tuxedos under blue skies.
Old lunchboxes layered in crusty grime,
Each a little mystery of snack time rhyme.

Socks with no pairs line the cobwebbed edge,
Uh-oh! Here comes Dad, we'll make a pledge.
To uncover a treasure from yesteryear,
Or maybe just find—my missing shoe here!

Laughter springs forth from the rooftop above,
A chorus of echoes that fit like a glove.
Let's search through the tiles, shake off the dust,
In this whimsy of life, it's laughter we trust.

Beneath the Ridge of Time

Up high where the sun paints the dust like gold,
Lies a storybook where adventures unfold.
A rubber band ball that once ruled the world,
Now rests in the corner, quietly twirled.

A slinky that once could do backflips with grace,
Now tangled in ribbons, what a silly case!
The clock has stopped, time's taken a leap,
Where giggles still echo, and secrets still keep.

A kite that got stuck in a tree rigid,
Once soared so high, now it's feeling frigid.
The roof's been a witness to laughter and cheer,
As we trace our past, finding everything dear.

Nostalgia weaves through the trusses and beams,
Mixed with the light of our childhood dreams.
With hearts full of joy, let's dance in this space,
Under the ridge where we once found our place.

Treasures Hidden in the Rafters

In the rafters, secrets hide snug and tight,
Like a game of peekaboo, out of sight.
A yo-yo forgotten beneath a shoe lace,
It swings to the rhythm of our childhood pace.

Old toys that squeak with a questionable squeal,
Engaged in a battle of how to conceal.
Magnifying glass for the curious eyes,
To see the small wonders that wear silly guise.

A baseball cap, sun-bleached and frayed,
Holds stories of summers, untroubled, displayed.
With paint and crayons enshrined on the floor,
We scribble our past, always wanting more.

Laughter and whispers twirl round the beams,
Treasure hunts hide in our magical dreams.
In this playful attic, we'll find what we seek,
With a wink to the future and giggles to speak.

The Resting Place of Dreams

In a shoebox, a dragon sleeps,
Worn-out socks its secret keeps.
A prize for laughter, a crown of cheese,
A cardigan hugging an old pet sneeze.

Napping on a cloud of fluff,
My sandwich is made of silly stuff.
A cat wearing glasses, oh what a sight,
Whiskers twitching, ready for flight.

Old toys gossip in silly rhymes,
Sharing secrets of forgotten times.
A bicycle dreams of zooming past,
But its wheels are flat, dreams won't last.

Memory flies on rubbery wings,
Chasing after those cartoon things.
In this attic of giggles, I must confess,
My dreams are as outlandish as my old dress.

Veils of Memory Crossed

A hat once worn by a chicken grand,
Decorated brightly with a rubber band.
It ran for office, a candidate bold,
Promising snacks for the young and old.

In a cupboard, cookies start to dance,
Twirling and spinning, given the chance.
Dip them in milk like they own the place,
Until one jumps out, oh what a race!

A forgotten diary with a cranky pen,
Whispers tales of what might have been.
Giggles erupt from each scribbled line,
Of aliens stealing my peanut butter brine.

Through these veils, the jester peeks,
With painted cheeks and ticklish cheeks.
Remembering moments in a clown's parade,
Where even the currant tart got laid.

The Chime of Inward Journeys

A bell on a tricycle rings so bright,
As I chase my shadows into the night.
With a sandwich hat and shoelace wings,
I explore the land of improbable things.

My thoughts bounce like a beach ball high,
Twisting and turning up in the sky.
A marshmallow elephant floats nearby,
With big goofy ears, waving goodbye.

In this inner realm where laughter grows,
Jellybeans mock what everyone knows.
A rubber chicken gives out advice,
On how to cook dinner with none of the spice.

Along the paths where giggles roam,
Curly fries shout, "Welcome home!"
Juggling memories, they tumble and sway,
As laughter returns, come what may.

Lullabies from Above

Clouds hum softly a tune so sweet,
While starlit pillows create a retreat.
An orchestra formed of donuts and tea,
Plays for the bears who dance with glee.

Chasing the fireflies with jelly-filled dreams,
While hiccuping frogs join in vibrant schemes.
Each giggle echoes through the moonlit sky,
As cupcakes take flight to flutter and fly.

A snuggle of kittens forms a warm nest,
Whiskers twitching, they giggle with zest.
Singing lullabies, the night cavorts,
While dreams reveal their fun little sorts.

Up in the heavens, fluffy and light,
Every memory dances, shining so bright.
With each gentle snore, the tales twirl and weave,
As midnight whispers, "We never leave."

Frayed Edges of Recollection

In corners, dust bunnies hop and play,
Old socks giggle in a time delay.
Forgotten snacks hide under the bed,
They come out dancing, just like I said.

A time machine made of teddy bears,
They'll take me back to my wildest flairs.
With every laugh, a memory sways,
As I chase my youth in a comical haze.

Bicycles rust with a wink and a grin,
Squeaky wheels hum of adventures within.
I wave to the neighbors from a dream,
They wave back, part of my wacky team.

In every frayed edge, stories unfold,
Laughing at the days, both embarrassing and bold.
Through giggles and snorts, I gather the fun,
Life's a jolly ride—let's go for a run!

The Space Where Time Meets Memory

Beneath the attic, where echoes reside,
A rubber chicken serves as my guide.
It tells tales of pies that flew through the air,
And neighbors who danced in mismatched underwear.

In this whimsical realm, I trip and I laugh,
Finding old photos of goofy giraffe.
Time bends here and grows ever thin,
As dancing dogs waltz with a toothy grin.

An umbrella spins like a merry-go-round,
With hidden treasures just waiting to be found.
Grandma's old hat does a jig as it sways,
While I try to recall my most awkward days.

Time slips and slides on banana peels,
Memories crackle, like unprocessed reels.
In this space, clowns and hats get along,
Reminding me where the funny belongs!

Cracks in Time's Ceiling

Up in the attic, I spot a big crack,
Where memories tumble and catch the whack.
A stuffed bear sneezes, what a silly sight,
As I tread through tales of joy and delight.

Old toys chatter, spinning funny yarns,
About pizza parties with rubbery barn swans.
Loud belly laughs echo through the rafters,
Unraveling tales of my youthful disasters.

Between old boards, shadows prance and sway,
To songs of the past from a lollipop day.
Cracks may be flaws, but they're portals, too,
To the great, wacky fun that I once knew.

With every glance, joy sneaks through the seams,
And I pluck at these memories, stretching my dreams.
As the cracks laugh back, it's clear to see,
Life's a comedic play, starring just me!

Light Filtering Through Past Windows

Sunbeams slip past, a tickling tease,
Warming the dust where my memories freeze.
Old cartoons flicker, dressed up in glee,
As I giggle at all that they used to be.

Laughter weaves in like a bold ballet,
Through windows that wobbly frame the day.
A fruitcake rattles, bizarre on the shelf,
With one ancient recipe cooked by myself!

In this bright glow, quirks come alive,
My rubber duck chorus begins to thrive.
As they chirp and they quack in resounding glee,
Turning the past into pure jubilee.

Light drips down like syrupy fun,
Memories are mushy, but aren't they a ton?
Let's toast to the silly, the goofy, the bright,
As laughter leaps high, like a kite in flight!

Ascent to the Unseen Past

I climbed a ladder made of dreams,
With squeaky rungs and silly themes.
Each step I took, a story peeked,
Of socks misplaced and laughter freaked.

The ghosts of snacks I used to crave,
In every corner, they misbehave.
A cookie jar with secrets old,
It spills its tales, both warm and bold.

My childhood toys have staged a coup,
They mock my age with games they brew.
A rubber duck starts quacking loud,
As I recall my goofy crowd.

The photos glare, with grins so bright,
Chasing butterflies till late at night.
I laugh at times I spilled my drink,
The silliest thoughts that make me wink.

Tresses of Time

In tangled locks, the moments hide,
A hairbrush lost, my secrets cried.
Each strand a tale of summers gone,
Popsicles and pranks, our childish con.

With every comb, a giggle's found,
A yo-yo's dance with laughter's sound.
The tangles weave a crafty plot,
Of treasure maps and battles fought.

Oh, how the curls would bounce and sway,
As I would dream of flying away.
The crazier styles, a sight to see,
My hair was wild, just like me!

In mirrors, looks of pure delight,
Reflecting joys of every night.
The hairstyles ruled, the laughs were grand,
With silly selfies, fingers planned.

Where Time Meets the Sky

I built a kite from yesteryear,
With paper scraps and endless cheer.
It soars up high, a flight to bliss,
Where clouds exchange a silly kiss.

Above the world, my past takes flight,
With goofy jokes and stars so bright.
The wind confesses, whispers sweet,
Of summer nights and friends we meet.

A comet zooms with laughter's grace,
Chasing memories in a wild race.
The moonlight giggles, swaying low,
As time and jest begin to flow.

With every gust, a memory dips,
Of ice cream faces and hand-made trips.
In this vast sky where time does play,
I find my youth in bright display.

The Archway of Youth

Beneath the arch where shadows twirl,
I danced to dreams, my heart a whirl.
Each stone, a giggle, every beam,
A playful wink, the silliest scheme.

I peeked through arches, eyes aglow,
As silly secrets dared to show.
The whispers echoed, light and loud,
Of paper planes and proud, lost crowds.

The swing set creaked, my feet took flight,
Launching laughter into the night.
A time capsule inside my head,
With bobbing heads and dreams unsaid.

Through that archway, I still can see,
The mischief wrapped in joy and glee.
With every step, I trace the past,
And cherish moments that will last.

The Space Where Dreams Dwell

In a corner, old socks stand,
Dancing alone, not quite planned.
They remember the feet they used to grace,
Now they just smile in this weird space.

A cat on a shelf with a judgmental glare,
He's plotting revenge with a flick of his hair.
Grandma's old lampshade spins tales that amuse,
Of wild parties where toast was refused.

On a chair, a brave donut takes charge,
Saying, 'I'm the life of the sweets entourage!'
But crumbs tell a tale that's far from divine,
Of evenings spent seeking the ultimate line.

In dreams, the old toaster starts to sing,
Its tunes lift the spirits, a magical fling.
As the kettle joins in with a bubbling cheer,
Together they laugh, 'Let's make breakfast here!'

Petals of the Past

A flower from high school, bright yet confused,
Wonders how it got so thoroughly used.
It flirts with old memories, sweet and absurd,
Each whispering secret, a giggle deferred.

Old photos hang crooked, they're smiling askew,
Captured in moments of wild rendezvous.
With bows on their heads, the group looks so fine,
Who knew those bright days would become punchlines?

There's a petal that warns, with a twitch of its stem,
"Don't wear bell-bottoms, they'll haunt you, my friend!"
Yet laughter erupts like the sun through the leaves,
As recollections bubble, like secrets up sleeves.

Caught in a breeze, the past sweeps away,
Follow it closely, it's here to play.
Watch out for the stumbles, giggles galore,
Life's just a garden, so come, let's explore!

Echoing Thoughts in the Rafters

Up in the attic, where shadows once danced,
Hats, coats, and memories, all seem entranced.
An old violin weeps a melodious tale,
While dust bunnies giggle, 'We'll never grow stale!'

Echoes of laughter bounce off the walls,
As shelves hold the trophies of great summertime brawls.
A rubber chicken perched on a box of old shoes,
Whispers to shadows the most scandalous news!

The cupboard creaks open, revealing a snack,
Cheese puffs and crackers in a colorful pack.
"Sneak a few bites—no one will see!"
For echoes of laughter just want to be free.

The rafters hold secrets, they've seen it all,
Love notes and blunders, both big and small.
Let's remember them fondly, with chuckles and cheers,
For life's just a play, with no room for fears.

A Summit of Silent Whispers

Atop a high mountain, where whispers converge,
Sit socks on a picnic, as shadows emerge.
They giggle and snicker at tales they once told,
Of adventures ridiculous and memories bold.

A sandwich atop peaks is a sight quite absurd,
With ants as the party, not caring - unheard!
They feast on the crumbs, plotting a spree,
While clouds let out roars, "We'll always be free!"

Beneath the blue sky, their laughter resounds,
Echoing softly as joy knows no bounds.
A summit where stories ascend like a kite,
In this whimsical world, every wrong feels just right.

So pack up your troubles and join the parade,
Where laughter's the currency we happily trade.
From socks to sandwiches, let good times unfurl,
For the peak of existence is one joyous whirl!

Threads that Bind the Past

In Grandma's attic, I found a shoe,
With glitter and gum, and a sock or two.
A cat in the corner, snoring so loud,
Dreams of fish feasts, where he's king of the crowd.

The old rocking chair creaks with delight,
As I tell it tales of mischief at night.
It chuckles and sways with every old jest,
A witness to history's comical quest.

There's a diary covered in dust and in grime,
With doodles and secrets that slip down through time.
Each page is a giggle, a slip, and a twirl,
A treasure trove of my childhood whirl.

And so I sit back, with a grin and a sigh,
As I weave through these threads, oh my, oh my!
With memories stitched tightly, a colorful blend,
In the fabric of laughter, where time has no end.

Nostalgic Corners of a House

In the corner sits a chair, threadbare, forlorn,
Where I plotted my heists as a mischievous scorn.
Next to it, a lamp with a shade that is cracked,
It flickers and blinks when I'm afraid I'm tracked.

The smell of old cookies still fills the warm air,
Though the cookie jar's empty, I didn't dare share.
The lingering echoes of laughter and fights,
Resounded through shadows of childhood delights.

There's a closet that creaks with secrets untold,
A sword made of cardboard that once seemed so bold.
I swish it around like I'm conquering lands,
And imagine the glory, as I make my demands.

So here in these corners, my heart takes a stroll,
Each nook holds a story, a piece of my soul.
And I chuckle and sing to the ghosts of my past,
In this house full of echoes, the moments will last.

Stars and Stories Above

Lying on rooftops, we counted the stars,
With wild dreams of planets and imaginary cars.
A spaceship made from blankets and dreams,
Zooming through cosmos, or so it all seems.

We'd giggle at aliens that danced on the moon,
While eating our snacks and humming a tune.
Each shooting star shattered our worries in flight,
As we shared our secrets beneath the soft night.

But then came the crickets with their boisterous song,
Interrupting our tales that had rambled too long.
We'd laugh at the racket, our laughter would swell,
In this theater of night, we crafted our spell.

So here's to the stars and the stories we spun,
To the laughter we shared, and the dreams we outrun.
In the vastness of midnight, our hearts all aglow,
The universe listened, and boy, did it know!

The Echo of Time's Canvas

In the attic of ages, I paint with a grin,
With colors of chaos and big messes within.
A canvas of memories, each shade full of fun,
Tiny moments of joy, like rain drops in sun.

There's a mishap with glue and a glittering mess,
As I sculpt silly figures in total distress.
A bear that forgot how to stand on two feet,
And a turtle in sneakers that dances to beat.

With every brush stroke, a tale finds its voice,
Of birthday surprises and toys of my choice.
I chuckle at pictures, both silly and bright,
Reflections of laughter, so pure, so light.

The echo of time calls me back to the start,
Where mischief and magic once painted my heart.
So I splash on some colors, and dance with my fate,
As I swim in this canvas, I find it's just great!

Memories Wrapped in Cedar

In a chest of cedar dreams,
Lies a sock that always seems,
To vanish with the last of light,
A mystery that sparks delight.

A squeaky chair, a woeful tune,
Dancing like a tipsy loon,
Grandpa's stories, always tall,
Made us giggle, made us fall.

Forgotten cake, a crazy mess,
Frogs that wore my Sunday dress,
Each summer's mishap, tales we spun,
Like fireflies under the sun.

Time's a prankster, never mild,
Always leaves us beguiled,
With each laugh a memory blooms,
In the attic, scents of looms.

Echoing Laughter Beneath the Slats

Beneath the beams, a sneeze awoke,
A mouse that danced with gentle yoke,
Tickles fade on splintered wood,
In every creak, a giggle stood.

A cat that stalked with stealthy paws,
Found her shadow in the jaws,
Of dreams still tangled in the night,
With silly purrs, she took her flight.

The echo of our giddy fits,
With echoes of forgotten skits,
Under slatted skies we'd scheme,
To catch the stars and start to dream.

Laughter woven between the lines,
In rows of jokes, as sun still shines,
Every whisper still enchants,
In our own nostalgic dance.

A Tapestry of Old Reflections

Threads of laughter, bright and bold,
Stories from the days of old,
A blanket stitched with warmth and care,
Memories linger everywhere.

An old dog on a sunny patch,
Who loved to nap, his favorite catch,
Each snore a tale of wild pursuits,
Chasing squirrels in plaid old boots.

My childhood bike with wiggly wheels,
Always gave me funny feels,
With pedals squeaky, laughter streamed,
In every turn, adventure dreamed.

Patchworked moments, sewn with glee,
A tapestry for us to see,
Navigating life's wide array,
With every joke, we found our way.

The Framework of My Journey

In the attic, a frame of cheer,
Puzzles missing one last piece here,
Cousins giggling as we try,
To fit a cat instead of sky.

Old photos hang with funky flair,
Why were pants so big back there?
Each snapshot giggles in the light,
Where time forgot to be polite.

Bumpy rides on homemade trains,
With lemonade and drippy rains,
Every bump a story bold,
In each adventure, laughter told.

The framework rests on silly schemes,
Built on bright and fragile dreams,
With each mishap, the journey grows,
A funny tale that still bestows.

Illumination of Silent Moments

In the attic where time seems to freeze,
Dust bunnies dance with the greatest of ease.
A sock puppet argues with an old shoe,
While a hat claims that it once flew too.

Light flickers on memories, clear yet absurd,
A rubber chicken is still quite disturbed.
Grandma's old photos, with faces so bright,
All wearing their glasses, yet squinting at light.

The clock's tick tock morphs into a tune,
As mice in the corner groove with a balloon.
Old toys peek out with their laughter and cheer,
While a forgotten jigsaw begins to appear.

Laughter bounces off cobweb-filled walls,
Each shadow a story in evening light calls.
In this silly gallery, both proud and shy,
I sneak a good giggle, then dash to the sky.

The Stories Held Up High.

Boxes piled high, reaching for dreams,
Containing the echoes of childhood schemes.
A scarecrow stands guard with a lopsided grin,
As kaleidoscope memories start to spin.

Whiskers belong to a sepia cat,
Who naps in the corner, completely flat.
Old board games whisper of nights full of fun,
As I trip over marbles in a silly run.

A dusty old bicycle waits for a ride,
It squeaks with secrets that it can't confide.
A record spins tales of disco delight,
While the vacuum sings opera, quite out of sight.

The ceiling's adorned with the oddest of things,
Like a rubber duck that announces it sings.
And here in this space, laughter spills from the past,
As memories flutter, forever amassed.

Echoes Under the Skylight

Under the skylight, the sunlight plays tricks,
As shadows perform their own little kicks.
A marching band of ants in a line,
Proudly parading, each ant looking fine.

Whispers of past games echo around,
While dust motes spin, like they're lost and found.
The old teddy bear holds a grudge with a frown,
For being forgotten when I left town.

The echoes of laughter bounce off the floor,
As I step on a toy, and it squeaks evermore.
Bright mismatched socks hang like flags in the sun,
Declaring a victory, oh what silly fun.

Up here in this chaos, joy surely flows,
Recalling the days of the highs and the lows.
With every old trinket, a chuckle resides,
In this attic of giggles where pure fun abides.

Whispers of Yesterday's Horizon

In corners where dust gathers stories once bright,
The tales of my youth still take delightful flight.
A paper airplane makes a daring escape,
While a stuffed bunny dreams of a grand landscape.

The jars filled with marbles spark flashbacks of glee,
Each one a memory, as round as can be.
From dodgeball disasters to rain-soaked gowns,
The echoes of laughter still dance in my crowns.

Old letters and postcards stick out like sore thumbs,
Vividly painted with whimsical sums.
An umbrella reminisces a day in the rain,
When we splashed in puddles, losing all sense of brain.

Stories like popcorn scatter in the air,
Tickling my senses, as I pause, stop and stare.
These whispers of joy that never quite fade,
In the attic of time, where my heart feels remade.

Threads of Time's Weave

Threads of laughter, spun with care,
A quilt of moments, light as air.
The cat's old tales, a tale or two,
With yarns so wild, they wear a shoe.

Sunshine spills on dusty shelves,
Where memories dance and play themselves.
A wig for dad, a hat for mom,
Stories bloom, and chickens drum.

In every nook, a giggle hides,
In socks mismatched, past joy resides.
Bubbles burst with goofy grins,
As time weaves on, this tale begins.

So come, my friend, let's weave and twine,
With silly threads, our hearts align.
A tapestry of laughs and cheer,
In every stitch, a memory dear.

Stories Nestled in the Attic

Up in the attic, dust and gold,
Where secrets linger, stories told.
A rocking horse with a fading grin,
Whispers of mischief dance within.

Grandma's shoes, a comical sight,
Too big to wear, yet full of light.
Old records spinning, voices soar,
As sock puppets plead for one encore.

A trunk of treasures, each a gem,
From Uncle Joe's flashy diadem.
Cousin's stories of dragons and fights,
Laughter echoes through the nights.

So let's climb high and take a peek,
At all the crazies we dare to seek.
In dusty corners, joy ignites,
With giggles shared under attic lights.

A Raft of Reminiscence

In a boat of nostalgia, we happily float,
With rubber ducks and an old toy goat.
Paddling softly through laughter's stream,
Chasing the remnants of a daydream.

Remember the summer in mom's big hat?
When ice cream melted and birds said, "chat."
We sailed through puddles that looked like seas,
With leaky boots and sticky knees.

The tall tales spun by a fanciful frog,
Who wore a crown made of an old soggy log.
Our minds drift on as the waves dance by,
In a raft of smiles, we laugh till we cry.

So grab your oars, let's row with glee,
On this silly journey, just you and me.
With memories rippling, we'll float along,
In our wacky boat where we both belong.

Tidal Waves of Remembering

Surfs up high with the tides of yore,
Waves of laughter crash on the shore.
A fish in my pocket—can you believe?
Or was it a prank, just meant to deceive?

In every splash, a joke takes flight,
As seagulls squawk with a comic bite.
Flip-flops squeak, and shorts ride high,
With sunburned noses, we wave goodbye.

The sandcastles built, a royal decree,
With candy crowns for all to see.
Our buckets overflow with giggles and cheer,
As we splash in memories tucked away here.

So ride these waves, let joy unwind,
In tidal love, we'll always find.
A shore of silliness stretched out wide,
With all our stories, happy and tied.

Tiles of Timeless Remembrance

In a patchwork quilt of thoughts, I dwell,
Each tile a story, some wise, some fell.
Grandma's tales of cats that wore shoes,
I laugh so hard, I spill my juice.

Under the sun, old jokes take flight,
Like squirrels in shorts, oh what a sight!
Stumbling over memories, I giggle and sway,
As ticklish nostalgia dances away.

Puzzles of mischief fly from the shelf,
Glued together by laughter, all by myself.
A misplaced sock hides stories untold,
In the attic of time, my treasures unfold.

Each tile a reminder, a version of me,
A patch of sunshine or a squirrel in a tree.
Sometimes I wonder, as I ponder this theme,
Are these tiles of laughter or just part of a dream?

The Gaze from Up High

Perched on a cloud, I spy a parade,
Of quirky moments that never quite fade.
A banana peel slip, a dog's wild dash,
I chuckle from above, while the ground goes splash.

Kites soar high with a tale to tell,
Of windy days and snacks that fell.
Hats blown away, oh the sight of delight,
As giggles and woofs mix in the light.

From my fluffy throne, I see the past,
Mismatched socks in a dance, oh so fast!
A board game beckons with pieces astray,
What's lost is found in a comical way.

So here I remain, with clouds all around,
Taking stock of the laughter in merry-go-round.
Each glance from above, a snapshot so spry,
The jester of memories waves up from the sky.

Dust and Memories in the Air

A sneeze of nostalgia, I'm blessed and perplexed,
As dust bunnies scatter, my thoughts they perplex.
Old toys come to life, with giggles and cheer,
The memories linger, they tug at my ear.

A rubber band war from days long ago,
When laughter was plenty, and time moved slow.
A feather duster fights with an old wooden chair,
"Dust me not, friend, I'm a relic with flair!"

I twirl with the specks of the yesteryears,
Each shimmer a tale, each laugh draws near.
Like popcorn in memory's delightful pan,
Every kernel of joy baked by the plan.

So let's raise a glass to the dust swirling round,
In the attic of laughter, where treasures abound.
For every sneeze triggers a giggle and smile,
Dusty and silly, it's worth every while.

Sheltered by Time's Embrace

Beneath a great hat, I find playful shade,
Where time's giggles echo, and games are played.
A umbrella of laughter, it shields and it warms,
As I dance through the years, weaving light-hearted charms.

In the breezy corners of yesteryears' bliss,
Popcorn and pranks, nothing amiss.
A caper or two with the socks on the run,
The wardrobe's a circus, oh what fun!

Jumbled encounters, like jigsaw pieces,
Fit together in smiles, as laughter increases.
A game of charades with my socks on the floor,
Each pose a portrait, who could ask for more?

So here I reside, in this whimsical space,
Playful uncertainties, a silly embrace.
With time as the driver and laughter the key,
I'm sheltered in joy, just my socks and me.

Beneath the Arc of Reminiscence

Underneath the sky so blue,
I recall a shoe stuck in goo.
Laughter echoes, a quirky thrill,
As I trip over my own will.

A sandwich dance from long ago,
With mayo high and mustard low.
My lunchbox became a treasure chest,
A feast of joy, a silly jest.

Family picnics, ants in gear,
Stealing crumbs, oh dear, oh dear!
Cousins giggle, falling down,
In this madness, I wear a crown.

Beneath the arc of time we play,
Chasing giggles in a silly way.
Time hops by on pogo sticks,
In this dance, we're all just kids.

Ghosts of Light and Shadow

In the attic, dust bunnies roam,
Whispers of jokes from a time long home.
A ghost with glasses, reading my grade,
Laughs as I stumble through a charade.

Shadows dancing in the late-night glow,
Twisting tales of my first grade show.
A chicken dance in a classroom bright,
Still makes me giggle, all through the night.

Echoes of laughter in the hall,
Tripping on shoes, oh, how I fall!
The ghost of a crayon scribbles my fate,
While drawings of dinosaurs just might wait.

Laughter lingers where memories play,
Each ghost appears to brighten the day.
In shadows we find the fun we seek,
Giggling, we dance, and rarely peek.

An Ascent into Memory Lane

Up on this hill where memories trot,
A yo-yo's saga—what a plot!
Zip through laughter, swing with glee,
As I attempt that old, wild spree.

Bright summer days with bikes that squeak,
Riding on roads where we once did leap.
Puddles splashed with water's grace,
Cackling loudly, our happy chase.

Hopping stones in the creek below,
Frog leaping left, a splash to show!
We made a ruckus, and oh, what fun,
A carnival ride under the sun.

Memory's ascent is wild and free,
Tumbling back to those carefree glee.
Smiles and giggles, the best of times,
In joy's sweet rhythm, life gently rhymes.

The Ridge of Reflection

Atop the ridge, I start to muse,
About a time I wore my shoes.
Inside out was the fashion of youth,
A style mishap—a silly truth!

I laughed so hard, I lost my hat,
Chased it down like a playful cat.
With friends beside, we made a scene,
Twirling 'round in grass so green.

Picnic days with ants that tease,
A blanket spread beneath the trees.
Sandwiches flying through the air,
Feeding birds is quite a dare!

At sunrise, we'd share silly tales,
Of pinecone boats and fairy trails.
Memories ride on laughter's wings,
In the ridge of life, joy still sings.

Lanterns in the Dust

In corners where the dust bunnies play,
I find shadows of laughter that sway.
Each light flickers with giggles so bright,
As memories dance in the dead of night.

Old socks that giggle on the line,
Tell tales of treasures, both yours and mine.
With lanterns aglow, the stories return,
In this funny world, there's much to learn.

Bouncing bags of mixed-up cheer,
I swear I keep finding my old career.
Lost in the closet, it trips on a shoe,
While I sit and ponder what day I blew.

With a sneeze and a wheeze, out pop the fun,
Memory gremlins just want to run.
They chase me around with their playful jests,
While I fall over my well-hidden chests.

Breezes Through Open Windows

The breeze sneaks in with a cheeky grin,
Whispers of laughter swirl and spin.
Curtains dance like they're in a race,
As memories giggle, finding their place.

A napkin holds secrets from meals long past,
And the fridge hums tunes so unsurpassed.
Oh, where are those socks? I'll leave it to chance,
A treasure hunt where lost things prance.

Inhaled aromas, a feast of the mind,
As echoes of joy swirl through the blind.
These breezes blow in strange foreign hues,
Tickling my nose with morning's good news.

Chasing the whiff of burnt toast once more,
As chuckles resound from the creaky floor.
The window swings wide, all cares blown away,
An open invitation to laugh and play.

Tattered Maps of Days Gone By

With maps frayed at the edges, clues run amok,
Where X marks the spot, I misplaced my sock.
Journey through laughter, you never can tell,
Which turn leads to treasures or just a bell.

A compass that spins in the oddest of ways,
Points me not north but to all of my plays.
Each crevice an echo of silliness found,
In tattered pages where memories abound.

Roaming through fields of pie-eating contests,
With only my chin and a cheeky jest.
And who knew a garden could hold such a laugh,
With carrots and radishes posing for p'graphs?

So here's to the maps, a whimsical guide,
To the silliness found in my daily stride.
As laughter leads me through winding old lanes,
Where joy and absurdity loosen their chains.

A Canopy of Faded Moments

Under the awning of once brilliant days,
Faded like jeans after countless sunrays.
Laughter hangs low, like fruit on the vine,
Each giggle and chuckle a well-aged fine wine.

Beneath umbrellas that twirl with delight,
I recall spilled ice cream on warm summer nights.
And here in the canopy, silliness reigns,
As nostalgia tickles my fanciful veins.

Old shoes peek out from a growing green egg,
Fish out memories with a gentle peg.
Whimsy grows strong in the shade of that tree,
Where laughter and sunlight dance wild and free.

So pillow fight clouds won't bat a bright eye,
As I chase after time like a kite in the sky.
Faded moments linger, with joy on the air,
Crafting a canopy that's always aware.

Fragments Lost in the eaves

Up in the attic, where dust bunnies play,
Old socks and toys tumble, hiding away.
A rubber duck laughs, with a crooked grin,
As if it knows secrets of where I've been.

A half-eaten cookie, a crumpled old hat,
Whispers of childhood, how silly is that?
The ghosts of my past dance with glitter and glee,
In this wacky collection, it's just me and me.

Old love notes stuck under a paint-peeling beam,
Worms of embarrassment gnaw at my dream.
With each crumb I find, oh what a delight,
To relive silly moments that tickled my sight.

So here's to the treasures, both weird and wild,
The laughter, the memories, of my inner child.
Each fragment a story, fractured but spry,
In the eaves of my mind, where the chuckles fly.

Memories Woven in Rafter's Embrace

Up high in the rafters, a tapestry grows,
With mischief and mayhem, all woven in prose.
A rubber band rocket, a missed birthday cake,
The giggles still echo, they're never opaque.

A dance with a broom to a song of my youth,
Made quite the impression, oh where is the truth?
And old polka dot shirts that once made me bright,
Now hang with disdain, oh where's the spotlight?

The cobwebs gather like secrets untold,
Each thread a reminder of memories bold.
From mud pies to mishaps, through laughter we stride,
In this funny old attic, where silliness hides.

So raise up a glass, to the high-flying fun,
To zany adventures that never are done!
Each rafter a witness, to moments so grand,
In this wacky wonderland, come take my hand.

Echoing Footsteps of Time

In the hallway, footsteps from ages ago,
Tiptoe behind me, just putting on a show.
Socks on the stairs, a slip and a slide,
I trip on my past, with a giggle inside.

There's an echo of laughter, an alligator grin,
As I dodge flying toys that come swooping in.
A party of memories, loud and absurd,
Play hide and seek, not a whisper nor word.

The echoing footsteps, they prance right through,
Unlocking the joy of the silly and true.
My home is a circus, oh what a delight,
With each bounding memory, like sprinkles, they bite.

To the rhythms of life, I cha-cha with glee,
As the footsteps behind me embrace and set free.
In this dance of nostalgia, let laughter unroll,
With each leap and tumble, I'm whole—oh so whole!

Beneath the Arch of Longing

Beneath a funny arch, where misplaced shoes dwell,
I find all the treasures, oh stories to tell.
Lost teddy bears chuckle, from days gone awry,
While socks hold a meeting, they're plotting to fly.

Wobbly tables hold secrets, like lemonade stains,
From lemonade stands run by kids with no brains.
A hat with a feather, a good luck charm too,
Flies off with the wind, oh what will it do?

Under the glow of this quirky old nook,
Each memory giggles, as if on the hook.
Puppies of yore bark, enchanting the scene,
With a symphony of smiles, oh what could it mean?

In this cozy corner where whimsy resides,
I weave all the laughter, with time as my guide.
So let's toast to the fumbles and moments gone wild,
Beneath the arch of longing, I'm forever a child.

Glimpses Through Gabled Reflections

In the attic, dust bunnies dance,
Chasing shadows with a funny glance.
Old photo frames with faces ask,
"Why so serious? Just lighten the task!"

A crooked hat hung up on the wall,
Winks at the cat who's ready to sprawl.
With each creak, the floorboards groan,
Sharing secrets in a quirky tone.

Spiders weave tales from threads of laughter,
While time itself just watches after.
A portrait grimaces, brushes aside,
Reminds me to embrace the silly side.

Gabled floors, stories to tell,
Of clumsy adventures that went quite well.
Each corner laughs at what's been lost,
In echoes of joy, we bear the cost.

When Time Tattered the Shingles

Shingles slipped like a tired old coot,
Whispering tales of fruit-flavored loot.
When Sundays had sun and Mondays did snooze,
Bumbling dances in mismatched shoes.

A wind chime clinks in a silly beat,
Reminds me of summers in candy heat.
Memories bubble like fizzy sodas,
Slurps and giggles in goofy odes.

Nails popped out, taking jabs at fate,
Loudly declaring, "Oh, don't you wait!"
The sky above tosses clouds of wit,
As we trip down memory lane—never quit!

With tattered shingles and funny-faced glee,
I skip through my past, so haplessly free.
Who knew that laughter could hold such sway?
A raucous echo, come what may!

The Eaves of Forgotten Laughter

Under the eaves, the whispers play,
With giggles that dance and sway.
A squirrel on the ledge does a silly caper,
Drawing memories like a comical paper.

Rain taps lightly, a rhythmic tease,
While we share secrets on knees and breeze.
Old shoes hang out, not wanting to go,
Collecting tales from long ago.

A hat with holes, like a cheese gone bad,
Cries out for someone who can't be sad.
With each drop of rain, a chuckle escapes,
Teasing the past, in funny shapes.

Forgotten laughter echoes around,
In corners where memories are profound.
Through the eaves, we shamble and roam,
Finding our joy in this delightful home.

Secrets Within Weathered Beams

The beams above hold stories tight,
Of pranks and giggles all through the night.
With every creak, an old friend calls,
"Remember the time we played inside the walls?"

A scattered chair, with legs askew,
Holds secrets of tossle (and maybe a shoe).
Old paintings smirk with a knowing grin,
As laughter spills out—let the silliness begin!

Dust settles lightly on memories dear,
While we reminisce with a hearty cheer.
A window's cracked, allowing the fun,
Through the years and beams, we've hardly begun.

So let's dance under this roof of dreams,
With all our laughter and silly schemes.
In the weathered beams, secrets will stay,
Tickling funny bones along the way!